THE SPEECH THAT MOVED THE WORLD

"HEGESIPPUS"

(Hugh J. Schonfield)

THE SPEECH THAT MOVED THE WORLD
"HEGESIPPUS"
(Hugh J. Schonfield)

Published for the Hugh & Helene Schonfield World
Service Trust
by

© 2023 Texianer Verlag
Tuningen Germany
www.texianer.com

ISBN: 978-3-910667-04-4

Originally Published 1932 by The Search Publishing
Company London

Dedicated
In Homage to the Kingliest of Men
and the Manliest of Kings

Front cover illustration:
Jesus Preaching the Sermon on the Mount
Gustave Dore (freechristimages.com)

"(Until the days of Trajan) the Church continued as a pure and uncorrupt virgin: whilst if there were any at all, that attempted to pervert the sound teaching of the Evangel of Salvation, they were yet skulking in dark retreats; but when the sacred choir of apostles became extinct, and the generation of those that had been privileged to hear their inspired wisdom had passed away, then also the combinations of impious error arose by the fraud and delusions of false teachers. These also, as there were none of the apostles left, henceforth attempted, without shame, to preach their false doctrine against the Evangel of Truth."

HEGESIPPUS (2ND CENTURY A.D.)

(Quoted by Eusebius, Eccl. Hist. Bk. III eh. xxii.)

CONTENTS

INTRODUCTION

CHAPTER I
THE BACKGROUND OF THE SPEECH — 13

CHAPTER II
THE SIGNIFICANCE OF THE SPEECH — 25

CHAPTER III
THE SPEECH ON THE MOUNT — 33

CHAPTER IV
OPENING REMARKS: BLESSINGS AND WOES — 41

CHAPTER V
THE PERMANENCE OF THE LAW — 45

CHAPTER VI
CONCERNING MURDER — 51

CHAPTER VII
CONCERNING ADULTERY — 57

CHAPTER VIII
CONCERNING OATHS — 61

CHAPTER IX
RETALIATION — 67

CHAPTER X
PUBLIC DEMONSTRATION OF PIETY — 75

CHAPTER XI
FAULT FINDING — 79

CHAPTER XII
FALSE PROPHETS — 83

CHAPTER XIII
CONCLUSION: SIMILE OF THE BUILDERS — 87

INTRODUCTION

The Church of Jesus was to be built upon a rock, but the doctrine of the Church is set upon two hills—the hill of Calvary and the hill of the Sermon. On Calvary was made the Atonement which set men free; on the Mount of Glad Tidings was proclaimed the Free State which should be their portion.

The Sermon on the Mount was the Church's charter, and we can quite understand the fact that the earliest quotations from the teaching of Jesus found outside of the Bible are taken from it. Throughout the centuries the Sermon on the Mount has stood for practical Christianity; it has been held up before peoples and princes as the ideal of human conduct. Its lofty moral tone, the nobility of soul which breathes in every line, has been an ensign to the nations. All the world has wondered, wondered and waited—to see a Christian; until a great sceptic should bitterly exclaim, "There has been only one Christian, and he was crucified."

After nearly two thousand years of Christianity, the world has agreed on its verdict, "The Sermon on the Mount is wonderful, but it is not workable." Its counsels are counsels of perfection, no nation or individual could live by such laws. They are more exacting than the laws of Moses which the Hebrews were unable to bear. Caught in the toils of its own unattainable virtues Christianity has struggled to qualify the sense of the expressions which fell from the lips of Jesus, to claim for them that they represented the principles not of the present but of a future ideal state of society. The words of the Sermon have been used and abused in controversy more, perhaps, than any other section of the Scriptures. "You call yourself a Christian, why don't you turn the other cheek?" has become the crude criticism of even the mildest remonstrance of a saintly soul.

No one denies the power of the Sermon for good. Thousands of holy lives testify to its redeeming influence. To its beneficent agency the world owes countless acts of loving-kindness and tender mercy. Its fruits are manifested in philanthropy and healing services, and in the self-restraint and gentleness which we call chivalry. If the supreme demands of the Sermon on the Mount have also produced hypocrites it is not because its standards are false, but because of the falsity of some Christian professions.

Commentary after commentary has been written on the Sermon on the Mount, sermon after sermon has been preached upon it, and yet to-day, the day when we need real Christianity most, its tenets appear so remote from actuality, so far removed from the strife and turmoil of this unquiet age, that there is a real danger of its passing into the limbo of discredited doctrines. It has ceased to stir and ceased to move, ceased to arouse any practical response. We have heard it too often. We have come to regard it as Sunday politics, entirely unrelated to the politics of the other six days of the week. We should smile at the idea of making its terms our platform for a general election. Imagine a Christian parliamentary candidate announcing to his constituents, "Ladies and Gentlemen, I have the honour to belong to the party of Jesus. If I am returned as your representative, I shall use my utmost endeavours to introduce his teaching into the affairs of this country." The result would be ludicrous. Christ at the bottom of the poll.

There was a time when the voice of the Nazarene was felt to have brought God down upon the earth and to have made Him the companion and confidant of man. But now that voice itself seems to have receded to an infinite distance, and we wait for a prophet to bring Jesus near again as Jesus once brought the Father Godhead. Meanwhile, earnest souls are attracted to Spiritualism and Theosophy and other cults, whose exponents seek to storm heaven that they may obtain direct guidance from some higher plane of living.

The world is harsh with failures, however much good they may have done in their better days. And it might seem that Jesus has failed, for the Kingdom of God which he promised has not yet materialised. A despairing clergy talks glibly of a Kingdom in the Heart, but no frittering away of the Gospels, no juggling with their plain message, can alter their anticipation of an external dominion of the Christ. To minimise this political aspect of the claims of Jesus is to acknowledge his defeat in the field where he confidently expected victory. The world has known many spiritual teachers of great power and insight: it has had and can have only one Messiah. It is this exalted office of Vicegerent of God on earth that differentiates the mission of Jesus from all others. There can be no question of comparison of Jesus with Moses or Buddha or Mahomet. He is the Christ, or he is an imposter. The Roman Catholic communion has held fast to this truth, even though it has failed to follow the Sermon on the Mount, and there is no provision in the New Testament for any temporary occupation of the Throne of David by a succession of Popes.

The Caesars knew what the Christian faith implied, and they arrested its adherents for treason. They may never have read the Apocalypse, but they realised that the Nazarenes bowed the knee to one whose name was written "King of kings, and Lord of lords."

The choirs still sing "Jesus shall reign where'er the sun doth his successive journeys run": the congregations still gabble "Thy Kingdom come"; but the worship of choir and congregation and minister is concentrated upon a semi-nude figure nailed to a beam of wood, a most unkingly figure, a very mockery of kingship. This is the vision before their eyes when they drink of the communion cup. They remember the words "This is my blood which is shed for many for the remission of sins," but they forget the triumphant "I will not henceforth drink of the fruit of the vine until I drink it new in my Father's king-dom." They leave the church as if they had partaken of a funeral feast, when they should be intoxicated with the privilege of hastening the Kingdom of God and of His Christ. Jesus sent forth his disciples not as apologisers but as ambassadors.

All these reflections do not leave us with the sorrowful conclusion that Jesus has failed, or that his faith was unjustified, but they do show that the Church has failed in forgetting the second fundamental function for which it was called into existence—the proclamation of the Kingdom of God. The Church has made Christianity into a religion and fashioned temples for its propagation, but Christianity was never intended to be a religion, it was a governmental system based on the principle of Divine Sovereignty. The Sermon on the Mount has lost its grip, and lost its meaning, largely because it is regarded as a sermon. There is still life and hope for the world in that great mountain speech. Now, when all kinds of remedies for the chaotic state of civilisation are being advocated, from Fascism to Communism, now is the time for the Church to return to its mission and proclaim a Theocracy. The Sermon on the Mount is practical politics, once it is released from theological misconceptions. A stricken world is waiting for authoritative guidance. The speech of Jesus in Galilee, infinitely more potent than Lincoln's at Gettysburg, offers the supreme solution to the Problems of the day. It is high time to transfer this speech with all its wealth of meaning from the pulpit to the press. Which newspaper will have the courage to be the first to give it proper Publicity?

If the slogan "Back to Christ" which is often heard has any value at all, let us be sincere and enter wholeheartedly into the mind of Jesus, and give honest consideration to his theocratic plan for world government.

The state of affairs which Jesus had to face in Palestine in the first Century is fundamentally the same as we are called upon to face to-day, and it is the object of this book to show the wisdom of his statesmanship in solving his contemporary problems as set forth in the Speech on the Mount.

If the Speech is properly understood there is no doubt that it can be, and should be, a rallying point for the world's best spirits. It should be possible, as Jesus intended, for all men of all creeds to be Christians—followers of the Messiah— without prejudice to the religion which they profess, whether they are Jews, Mahometans, Buddhists or Hindus. "Let every man abide in the same calling wherein he was called" (1 Cor. vii. 20). Kipling has said that "East is East and West is West, and ne'er the twain shall meet." But this is not true. Socially, politically, economically and spiritually, they can meet in Christ. He has broken down the middle wall of partition in a sense far transcending mere theological distinctions. He will yet be justified of his faith that "I, if I be lifted up, will draw all men unto me."

THE SPEECH THAT MOVED THE WORLD

CHAPTER I

THE BACKGROUND OF THE SPEECH

The faults of most otherwise admirable attempts to interpret the teaching of Jesus have lain in the inability of those who undertook the task to recapture the spirit of the age in which he lived. In order to understand the Gospels aright there is required an intimate acquaintance with other documentary sources, religious and political, dealing with the period under survey. Further, the would-be historian of Christian beginnings must dispense both with the vestments of the ecclesiastic and the motley of the sceptic and assume the mantle of the prophet. Above all is required an inside knowledge of, and heart-felt sympathy with, the Jewish people in their struggle for independence, and their belief in divine intervention to secure their deliverance from the burdensome oppression of alien tyranny on the one hand, and the yoke of an apostate and corrupt sacerdotalism on the other.

Among the few who have successfully fulfilled these conditions is Edward Holton James. In a little-known work published under the title of *The Trial before Pilate*, he has depicted with accuracy and graphic eloquence the political situation in Palestine as Jesus found it.

"The government in Jerusalem was a despotism," writes James, "and Pilate was the despot. On the one hand were the chief priests who were maintaining that despotism. On the other hand were the Jews who were looking for redemption in Israel, the great multitude of the common people... These were the opposing parties. To exist or not to exist as a nation— that was the question. That was the vital issue. The outlook was very gloomy for the children of Israel. There was not any hope left for this poor, broken-hearted, captive people... But at the very moment when the outlook was darkest a man appeared to show the way. He brought a message from Jehovah. The voice of a prophet was again heard in Israel. This man was clothed with the authority of the invincible and eternal God. God lived. Hope revived. sorrow and despair gave place to gladness. Portents and wonders were seen in the heavens. Shepherds watching their flocks by night saw the angel of the Lord. A mighty shout of joy went up from all the children of the Jews:

"Blessed be the Lord God of Israel, for he hath visited and redeemed his people!" (pp. 184-185).

Speaking of the conditions under which Jesus taught, James says: "When a man is asked a question, and he knows that if he answers that question in a certain way he will be punished by death, he does not enjoy freedom of speech. Jesus was in the centre of conflict. He was surrounded by dangers of which no modern speaker can have any conception. He was parrying the thrusts of the enemy. He was defending at that moment the cause of the nation which had no rights. He himself had no rights, as rights are understood to-day... He had no right to speak at all. He spoke only be-cause he had the protection of the multitude. The multitude was on his side. The authorities were on the other side. An armed truce existed between the multitude and the authorities. The slightest advantage taken of that truce by one side or the other was sufficient to precipitate civil war" (p. 27).

Christians have for so long looked at the great tragedy through the medium of devotional commentaries that they have been blind for generations to the real relationship of Jesus to his times. Who can enter into the unfathomable grief which made even his brave spirit break down in bitter tears as he gazed on Jerusalem, his own dear Jerusalem, so far fallen, so heedless of the tide which was inevitably sweeping her and her children to destruction.

For those who have eyes to see and ears to hear, the Gospels are full of the social circumstances amidst which Jesus lived. The evangelists reveal an economic state of affairs which could hardly be worse, squalor, poverty and disease among the tax-burdened populace; excessive riches and overbearing insolence among the nobility and unscrupulous profiteers. A brief glance at the available material may do more to correct false impressions than a host of generalisations.

A man who could not pay his lord the exorbitant dues and taxes was liable to be sold with his wife and children to defray the debt (Matt, xviii. 25). The poor widow, whose little livelihood has been taken away, has to deal with an unjust judge who fears neither God nor man, and has no other means of redress than her importunity (Luke xviii. 1-5). Tax collectors extort unlawful revenues (Luke xix. 8), while the rich nobleman, hated for his hardness, goes off to enjoy himself in foreign lands, leaving his underlings to amass money for him the best way they can in his absence (Luke xix. 12-17). The self-satisfied capitalist decides to retire on his gains (Luke xii. 16-21). The plutocrat feasts sumptuously in his palace, caring nothing for the beggar covered with sores lying at his gates (Luke xvi. 19-31). In a mental stupor by reason of their privations, the common people follow any bene-factor about like dogs (Matt. ix. 35-38; xiv. 13, etc.), and bring their sick folk for healing (Matt, iv. 23-25; xv. 30-31, etc.). False prophets trade on the people's misery (Matt. vii. 15-16), On the slightest sign of disaffection the conquerors cut down the people in cold blood, even when engaged in worship (Luke xiii. 1-2). Reformers and patriotic preachers are arrested, and more often than not executed (Matt. x. 16-39) Faithful souls run grave risks in giving such persons shelter (Matt. x. 40-42). Spies and informers abound, and mingle with the crowds waiting to catch some word of antagonism to the authorities (Matt. xiii. 9-13), or ask pointed questions involving political issues (Matt. xv. 15-21). The authorities are in continual fear of popular risings (Matt. xxvi. 5).

These references disclose the real meaning of sayings of Jesus such as the following:

THE BACKGROUND OF THE SPEECH 17

"Come unto me, all ye that labour and are heavy laden, and I will give you rest."

"The foxes have holes, and the birds of the air nests; but the Son of Man hath not where to lay his head."

"Behold I send you forth as sheep in the midst of wolves: be ye therefore subtle as serpents, and simple as doves."

"If any man will come after me, let him deny himself, and take up his cross daily, and follow me."

On turning to the pages of Josephus, the Jewish historian of the time, the accuracy of the impression created by a study of the Gospels is fully borne out. A few extracts may help to supplement the statements of the evangelists.

"And thus did a great and wild fury spread itself over the nation, because they had no king to keep the multitude in good Order; and because those foreigners, who came to reduce the country to sobriety, did, on the contrary, set them more in a flame, because of the injuries they offered them, and the avaricious management of their affairs" (Antiq. XVII. x. 6).

Recording the reception of the Roman census in the reign of Archelaus, about twenty years prior to the public ministry of Jesus, Josephus writes: "Yet there was one Judas, a Gaulonite, of a city whose name was Gamala, who, taking with him Zaddoc, a Pharisee, became zealous to draw them to a revolt, who said that this taxation was no better than an introduction to slavery, and exhorted the nation to assert their liberty;... a famine also coming upon us, reduced us to the last degree of despair, as did also the taking and demolishing of cities" (Antiq. XVIII. i. 1).

Among other causes which contributed to the general disaffection was the policy pursued by the Herodian princes of paganising Palestine. Herod I, called the Great, had initiated this policy. Again to quote Josephus: "Herod revolted from the laws of his country and corrupted their ancient constitution, by the introduction of foreign practices;... for, in the first place, he appointed solemn games to be celebrated every fifth year in honour of Caesar, and built a theatre at Jerusalem, as also a very great amphitheatre in the plain... He also made proclamation to the neighbouring countries, and called men together out of every nation. The wrestlers, and the rest of those that strove for the prizes in such games... And truly foreigners were greatly surprised and delighted at the vastness of the expenses here exhibited; but to natural Jews this was no better than a dissolution of those customs for which they had so great a veneration" (Antiq. XV. v. 1).

It was this Herod who began to turn many of the Palestinian villages into towns on the Greek model, renaming them after the Roman emperor and his relatives. Each of such towns, of course, contained temples in which sacrifices were offered in honour of Caesar. Thus Samaria was rebuilt and called Sebaste in honour of the empress and Strato's tower was renamed Caesarea. Herod the tetrarch, and his brother Philip, followed in the footsteps of their father. The first elevated the village of Betharamphtha to the dignity of a city, and called it Julias, after the empress, while Philip, in his turn, changed Bethsaida into Caesarea Philippi, and Paneas into Julias, after the emperor's daughter.

Jesus refused to recognise these places by their pagan names; he vigorously denounced the corruption of the Graecised cities. "Woe unto thee, Chorazin! Woe unto thee, Bethsaida!... And thou, Kapharnaum, which art exalted to the heavens, shalt be brought down to hell." He likens them to Tyre and Sidon, Sodom and Gomorrah, below whose moral level they had sunk. The "wise and the prudent" Herodian politicians were blind to the claims of God on the national life; only the "babes" of the common people accepted the Divine Sovereignty.

Turning from the Herodians to the high priestly party, the Sadducees, another side of the painful picture presents itself. In this domain Annas, or Hannan, was the prime mover. The Gospels, Josephus, the Talmud and Jewish apocalyptic writings reveal the manner in which the temple of God had become a "den of robbers." Here it will suffice to describe briefly the situation as Jesus found it.

The Temple in those days received enormous revenues from the offerings of Jews, which were sent from all parts of the world. Cicero, in his defence of Flaccus, says: "We come now to that famous cause of grumbling, the gold of the Jews... Seeing that the Jews were exporting gold annually from Italy and all the provinces to Jerusalem, Flaccus prohibited this exportation from Asia. Who would not sincerely praise this measure?... Resistance to a barbarous superstition was a mark of energy on the part of Flaccus" (Pro Flacco, 28). There is a curiously modern ring about this. When Herod and Agrippa were visiting Ionia, the Jews of those parts laid a Petition before them for the restoration of their Privileges, which were being abused. Among these they mentioned that they "were deprived of the money they used to send to Jerusalem." Josephus records that during an insurrection in the days of Archelaus, "the Romans also rushed through the fire (into the Temple)... and seized on that treasure where the sacred money was deposited: a great part of which was stolen by the soldiers" (Antiq. XVII. x. 2). At another time Pilate caused a riot by appropriating some of the sacred money for the purpose of building an aqueduct to bring water into Jerusalem. So much did this vast treasure awe the minds of the people that a man who had sworn by the Temple alone was considered free of his oath; but if he had sworn by the gold of the Temple he was bound to his oath (Matt, xxiii. 16-17).

In order to exchange the money thus brought by pious Jews, which often bore representations of heathen gods, for the sacred shekel of the Sanctuary, money changers sat in the outer court at festival times for the purpose. This legitimate proceeding was, however, taken full advantage of by the chief priests, to whom a share in the commission charged became an additional source of revenue. Other charges were made for certifying the physical fitness of animals brought up for sacrifice; and from those who had come long distances, high prices were extracted for the sale of these on the spot. Jesus had the whole-hearted sympathy of the people when he overturned the tables of the money changers and the stalls of the dove sellers, and bade them "Take these things hence;

make not my Father's house an house of merchandise" (John ii. 15-16).

Such was the state of friction between the people and the authorities, Jewish and Roman, that the Procurators found it necessary to bring up reinforcements of soldiers to quell any popular outburst that might be made at the festivals. If one were to ask what thoughts were uppermost in the minds of the multitudes at this period, one would receive a threefold answer: (1) Food, for the people were often starving: (2) Longing, for God's miraculous intervention in their dire need: (3) Conviction, that the proud heathen would yet be subject to a redeemed Israel. It was on these three counts that Jesus was tempted of the devil.

When all the facts which have been enumerated are taken into consideration, it becomes evident to the impartial investigator that Christianity in its inception was not a new religion, but an integral part of the great Jewish patriotic and theocratic movement, brought about by so many contraventions of national and religious rights, which took its rise in those days among the Palestinian country folk, particularly in Galilee. It was no ordinary political movement, for its avowed object was the establishment of the Kingdom of God on earth.

From this viewpoint, when it is recognised that the mind of Jesus was continually revolving the problem of his people's sufferings, it becomes easier to understand his expression of such sentiments as, "I am not sent but unto the perishing sheep of the house of Israel" (Matt. xv. 24). And when he sought to define the mission with which he felt himself charged, he could only quote the words of the prophet: "The spirit of the Lord is upon me, because he hath anointed me to preach glad tidings to the poor; he hath sent me to heal the broken-hearted, to proclaim deliverance to the captives, and recovering the sight of the blind, to set at liberty them that are bound, to proclaim the acceptable year of the Lord" (Luke iv. 18-19).

It is from this viewpoint that we shall seek to understand the Speech on the Mount.

"When Jesus came," says James, "he brought freshness of thought into a world that was jaded and stagnant and hopeless. It was the freshness of morning dew and of summer showers... He inspired his friends and companions by his magnificent daring, by his matchless leadership. In him they saw David going to meet Goliath. In him they saw Moses giving the law to the people. They stood in speechless wonder as they beheld this young Galilean, without sword or shield, defy the mailed power of the Roman Empire. Here was a man who gave his life for truth. The blows which he delivered were terrible, and before him his enemies staggered and reeled. It was God himself who had taken the form of a man, and whose tongue, like a blade of tempered steel, cut down the lies and hypocrisy of the age" (p. 27).

CHAPTER II

THE SIGNIFICANCE OF THE SPEECH

In this chapter we shall deal with the significance of the Speech on the Mount both for Jesus himself and for the compiler of Matthew's Gospel who undoubtedly represented a very large body of early Christian opinion.

Biblical critics seem to spend a great deal of time in minding their P's and Q's (P. is the Priestly document discerned in the Pentateuch, while Q., standing for Quelle—German, "Source" —is a hypothetical document to account for common matter in Matthew and Luke which cannot be traced to Mark). This kind of literary analysis, however, is not conducive to a sound historical exegesis, and no use will be made of it in the present work. No great critical acumen is necessary to realise the fact that the Speech as it stands in Matthew is not a continuous discourse. The framework is an address of special importance delivered by Jesus on a particular occasion, as indicated in the Gospels of Matthew and Luke. But into this framework, in Matthew at any rate, a number of sayings spoken at other times have been inserted at different points to swell its bulk. These include the so-called Lord's Prayer and a complete speech addressed to the disciples privately (Matt. vi. 19-34; Luke xii. 12-31).

Why did the compiler of Matthew's Gospel wish to extend the Speech to so great a length? It occupies a larger space than the story of the Passion. The reason does not seem to be that he could think of nowhere better to put these sayings, but that for him the basic Speech had a significance which he desired to emphasise. It was as much a landmark in the life of Jesus as the Baptism, the Transfiguration and the Crucifixion: it signified nothing less than his public assumption of the office of Messiah.

When Jesus was baptised by John the anticipation in his own mind that he might be the Messiah became a certainty. The Spirit of the Lord had rested upon him. God had accepted him that day as His beloved son. This, the so-called Adoptionist doctrine, is certainly the original one. According to early authorities (the Epistle to the Hebrews, the Gospel of the Hebrews, the MSS. Codex D and the Old Latin at Luke iii. 22, Justin Martyr, Clement of Alexandria, etc.) the heavenly voice proclaimed, "Thou art my son; this day have I begotten thee" (Psalm ii. 7). The primitive Jewish Christians believed that Jesus became the Messiah, the Son of God, at his baptism (cf. Matt. xvi. 16, John vi. 69, Matt. xxvi. 63, Mark xiv. 61, Luke iv. 41, John xi. 27, xx. 31). The kings of the ancient nations styled themselves Sons of God as being the representatives on earth of the national deity. The Jewish kings were no exception (II Sam. vii. 14, I Chron. xvii. 13-14, Psalm lxxxix. 26-27, etc.). There was no suggestion of eternal pre-existence in this conception of divine sonship.

This truth is more fully brought out in the primitive Hebrew Gospel, quoted by Jerome in his commentary on Isaiah xi. 2. "The whole fountain of the Spirit descended and rested upon him (Jesus), and said to him:

My son, in all the prophets was I waiting for thee that thou shouldst come, and I might rest in thee. For thou art my rest, thou are my first-begotten son, that shall reign for ever."

It was believed that the gifts of the Spirit of God mentioned in this verse of Isaiah were given severally to the prophets but entirely (the whole fountain of the Spirit) to the Messiah. Justin Martyr explains: "The Scripture says that these enumerated powers of the Spirit have come upon him (Jesus)... because they would rest in him... For the prophets, each receiving some one or two powers from God, did and spoke the things which we have learned from the Scriptures... Solomon possessed the spirit of wisdom, Daniel that of understanding and counsel, Moses that of might and piety, Elijah that of fear of the Lord, and Isaiah that of knowledge; and so with the others.... Accordingly he (the Spirit) rested when he (Jesus) came" (Dialogue with Trypho lxxxvii).

We are here in touch with the great test for claimants to the Messiahship. Isaiah xi. 2-5 is regarded already as a proof passage in the pre-Christian Book of Enoch. It is there stated (xlix. 2-4): "The Elect One is mighty in all the secrets of righteousness, and unrighteousness will disappear as a shadow, and have no continuance, because the Elect One standeth before the Lord of Spirits, and his glory is for ever and ever, and his might unto all generations. And in him dwells the spirit of wisdom and the spirit of Him who gives knowledge, and the spirit of understanding and of might and the spirit of those who have fallen asleep in righteousness. And he will judge the secret things and no one will be able to utter a lying word before him; for he is the Elect One before the Lord of Spirits according to His good pleasure."

When Barcochba (A.D. 133-135) claimed to be the Messiah, the Rabbis replied: "It is written of the Messiah (Isaiah xi. 3), that he shall be of quick understanding to discern the good: canst thou do this? When they saw he could not, they slew him" (Sanhedrin 93b). The whole life of Christ shows how he passed this test successfully.

After the Baptism, the Spirit drove Jesus into the wilderness, where he wrestled with Satan for the symbolic forty days on the manner of his Messiahship. Then he went forth, not yet to teach "as one having authority of his own," but echoing the message of the Baptist: "Repent ye, for the Kingdom of Heaven is at hand."

"In the power of the Spirit" Jesus returned from Judaea into Galilee, and there, first, in his own synagogue at Nazareth, gave himself out to be the Messiah to the great offence of his townsfolk, who found it impossible to associate the son of their neighbour Joseph with so high a dignity. The next step, in spite of this rebuff, was to make the same declaration before all Israel. Jesus testified "that a prophet hath no honour in his own country." It would not be so with the nation at large. Already his fame had spread abroad, and great crowds from Galilee, Judaea, the Decapolis, Peraea and the sea coast, in fact geographically from every part of Palestine, were flocking to hear him.

The great moment had come. On a mountain-side near Kapharnaum Jesus took his stand, and in the Speech on the Mount set forth his Messianic policy to his followers and the assembled people. It was his speech from the throne. Before him were representatives of every class and every part of the Land of Israel, who would carry away his words, and upon whose allegiance his ultimate success would depend. Jesus was equal to the occasion. In eloquent language, with a masterly grasp of the political, religious and economic conditions then prevailing, and with a perfect understanding of the psychology of his audience, Jesus delivered perhaps the greatest speech ever made by man.

Failure to recognise the true significance of the Speech, as here indicated, has produced numberless misapplications of its terms, and has given rise to the groundless charge of im-practicability levelled against its teaching. The times, the audience and the occasion must be properly understood before the expositor is free to pronounce judgement on the meaning of any statement. Whatever Jesus said was forceful and appropriate, intended to guide the conduct of his hearers individually and collectively in the peculiar circumstances in which they, and they alone, were placed. If we can apply to ourselves any part of the message, that must be taken as wholly apart from the objects of the speaker. What has in effect become a sermon to us was something very different to the assembly at the foot of the mount.

In both the Gospels of Matthew and Luke (Matt. iv. 24-25, Luke vi. 17) the Speech is introduced by a description of a great multitude of people out of all parts of the country drawn by the fame of Jesus to seek healing for their bodily and spiritual ailments. This was the audience. What of its quality? Dr. Joseph Klausner, who has made a life-study of the period, supplies the answer in his Jesus of Nazareth. "Owing to protracted wars and tumults and the terrible oppression of Herod and the Romans, Palestine, and especially Galilee, was filled with the sick and suffering and with those pathological types which we now label neurasthenics and psychasthenics. The disturbances had multiplied the poor, the impoverished and the unemployed, with the result that in Palestine and... again, particularly in Galilee (since it was far removed both from the centre of civil rule and from saner spiritual influences), such 'nerve cases'—dumb, epileptics, and the semi-sane—were numerous" (p. 266). Again, "Palestine thus came to possess a class of poor, destitute and unemployed, and landless peasants, side by side with a class of wealthy farmers, great landed proprietors and rich bankers. The former waxed poorer and poorer, sinking into mendicancy, crushed and depressed, hoping for miracles, filling the streets of town and village with beggary and piety or (in the case of the more robust) with brigandage, highway-robbery and revolt; outcasts, haunting the caves and desert places and the rocks and crevices of the mountains" (p. 189).

With such an audience as this anything but a message calculated to illumine the immediate and vital problems would fail of its purpose. With too many pulpit sermons the criticism is often justly made that the speaker is out of touch with realities; the sentiments expressed are elevated and beautiful and true; but they do not sink home because the state of mind of the hearers does not predispose them to apprehend what is said. Many people have a picture-book impression of the Christ with two fingers uplifted talking eternal verities over the heads of a number of awe-stricken rustics. How false this picture is. Jesus made no such blunder. Guided by the history of the past, possessed of a keen insight into the terrible conditions of the present, actuated by the highest patriotic and moral motives, and with an unbounded faith in the promises of God, he gave to his generation his wise and considered advice, the fruit of many years' earnest thought. He addressed himself to matters that were in every mind there present, he dealt with grievances that cried to heaven for redress, with crooked souls and warped spirits that needed to be made straight before they could enter the Kingdom of God.

CHAPTER III

THE SPEECH ON THE MOUNT

It has already been remarked that the discourse is a great speech. Perhaps it has been regarded too little from this point of view. Its structure shows the working of a logical mind. The oratorical devices used exhibit a fine command of language and a profound knowledge of human psychology. From the pithy and pointed beatitudes and denunciations, designed to attract and attach the interest of the audience, to the appropriate closing simile of the wise and foolish builders, every moment is intense, every pronouncement is of weighty import. It is unfortunate that we cannot be absolutely sure of the text of the Speech; some adjustments in the course of the compilation were unavoidable. But by excluding from the Matthean Version those passages which occur in other and more appropriate contexts in Mark and Luke, and by a comparison of the remaining sections with the Lukan version, it is possible to arrive at a fairly reliable definition of its contents. The text itself shows that Matthew gives the correct sequence. By applying these rough but reasonable criteria, and taking Matthew as a basis, the extent of the Speech is seen to be Matthew v. 3-12, 17-24, 27-28; vi. 1-8, 16-18; vii. 1-5, 12, 15-21, 24-27. Read thus, the Speech contains no irrelevancies and develops in an orderly manner, each new subject arising naturally out of the previous one. The heads of the Speech are as follows:

1. Opening Remarks (Blessings and Woes).
2. The Permanence of the Law.
3. Concerning Murder.
4. Concerning Adultery.
5. Concerning Oaths.
6. Retaliation.
7. Public Demonstrations of Piety.
8. Fault Finding.
9. False Prophets.
10. Conclusion (Simile of the Builders).

These ten heads represent the progress of thought in the mind of Jesus on that memorable occasion, and it will be the object of the commentary to consider their appropriateness and essential meaning for the audience to whom they were addressed. The exposition is neither a devotional nor an exegetical one as these terms are usually applied, yet in its special intention it holds something of both. What is given here for the first time is the action in conjunction with the atmosphere, so that the reader if he has any imagination can find himself among the audience of the Speech and apprehend the true import of the message.

The Speech On The Mount

Happy are ye O poor! for yours is the kingdom of Heaven.

Happy are ye that hunger now! for ye shall be filled.

Happy are ye that weep now! for ye shall laugh.

Happy are ye, when men shall revile you, and persecute you, and shall say all manner of evil against you falsely, for the Son of Man's sake! Rejoice and be

glad! for great is your reward in heaven: for so did
their fathers unto the prophets.
But woe unto you that are rich! for ye have received
your consolation.
Woe unto you that are full now! for ye shall hunger.
Woe unto you that laugh now! for ye shall mourn and
weep.
Woe unto you, when all men shall speak well of you!
for so did their fathers to the false prophets.

Think not that I am come to annul the Law or the
Prophets: I am not come to annul, but to fulfil. Verily I
say unto you, Till heaven, and earth pass away, one yod
or one hook shall in no wise pass away from the Law, till
all be fulfilled. And whosoever shall annul one of these
least commandments, and shall teach men so, shall be
called least in the kingdom of Heaven. And I say unto
you, Unless your righteousness shall exceed the righteousness of the Pharisees and Scribes, ye shall not enter
into the kingdom of Heaven.

Ye have heard what was said to the ancients, Thou shalt
not murder; and whoso committeth murder shall be condemned to the judgement. But I say unto you, That whosoever shall be enraged against his brother shall be
condemned to the judgement. And whosoever saith unto
his brother, Raca! shall be condemned to the council of
the synagogue. And whosoever saith unto him, Moreh!
shall be condemned to the fire of Gehenna. And if thou
present thine offering at the altar, and there rememberest
that thy brother hath ought against thee; leave there thine
offering before the altar, and go thou first and atone to
thy brother, and then come and present thine offering.

Ye have heard that it was said to the ancients, Thou shalt not commit adultery. But I say unto you, That whosoever seeth a woman and lusteth for her hath already committed adultery with her in his heart. And if thy right eye offend thee, pluck it out, and cast it from thee: for it is better for thee that one of thy members should perish, than that thy whole body should be cast into Gehenna. And if thy right hand offend thee, cut it off, and cast it from thee: for it is better for thee that one of thy members should perish, than that thy whole body should be cast into Gehenna. It was also said concerning him that would put away his wife, that he should write her a bill of divorcement, and give it unto her, and send her away from his house. But I say unto you, That whosoever shall put away his wife, saving for the cause of fornication, causeth her to commit adultery: and whosoever taketh her that is cast off committeth adultery.

Again, ye have heard that it was said to the ancients, Thou shalt not forswear thyself, but shalt pay unto the Lord thy vow. But I say unto you, Ye shall not swear by a confirming word; neither by heaven, for it is God's throne; nor by the earth, for it is the footstool of His feet; neither by Jerusalem, for it is the city of the great king. Neither shalt thou swear by thy head, in that thou hast no power to whiten one hair or to turn it black again. But let your words be, Yea, yea; Nay, nay: for whatsoever is more than these words is of evil.

Ye have heard what was said, An eye for an eye, a tooth for a tooth. But I say unto you, That ye withstand not evil: but if one would smite thee on the right cheek, turn unto him the other also. And him that taketh from thee

THE SPEECH ON THE MOUNT

thy coat, let him have thy cloak also. And him that impresseth thee for one mile, go with him even twain. And whoso asketh of thee give to him, and of him that taketh away thy goods, ask them not again.

Ye have heard that it was said, Thou shalt love thy neighbour, and hate thine enemy. But I say unto you, Love your enemies, do good to them that hate you, and pray for them that persecute you and despitefully use you; that ye may become the children of your Father which is in heaven, who maketh His sun to rise on the good and on the evil, and sendeth rain on the righteous and on the wicked. For if ye love only them which love you, what reward have ye? Do not even transgressors do this? And if ye ask after the peace of your brethren only, what do ye exceed? Do not even the Gentiles do this? Be ye therefore perfect, like your Father which is in heaven, who is perfect.

See that ye bestow not your alms before me, so that they may see you: for then ye have no reward of your Father which is in heaven. Therefore when thou bestowest alms, blow not a trumpet before thee like the hypocrites do in the synagogues and in the streets, in order that men may honour them. Verily I say unto you, Already they have received their reward. But thou, when thou dispensest alms, thy left hand shall not know what thy right hand doeth: that thine alms may be in secret, and thy Father which seeth in secret shall Himself recompense thee in public.

And be not like the hypocrites when thou prayest: for they delight to stand in the assemblies and at the corners of the streets to pray, that men may see them. Verily I say unto you, Already they have received their reward. But thou, when thou prayest, enter into thine apartment, and shut thy door, and pray to thy Father which is in secret; and thy Father which seeth in secret shall recompense thee in public. And ye, when ye pray, multiply not words like the Gentiles do; who think that in an abundance of words they shall be heard. But be ye not likened unto them; for your Father knoweth what is needful for you, before ye ask Him.

And ye, when ye fast, be not like the hypocrites: for they begrime and disfigure their faces, that they may appear in the sight of men to fast. Verily I say unto you, Already they have received their reward. But thou, when thou fastest, anoint thine head, and wash thy face, that thou appear not unto men to fast, but unto thy Father which is in secret, who shall Himself recompense thee in public.

Judge not, and ye shall not be judged: condemn not, and ye shall not be condemned. For with what judgement ye judge, ye shall be judged: and with what measure ye mete, it shall be measured to you again.

And how seest thou the splinter in thy brother's eye, but seest not the beam that is in thine own eye? And how sayest thou to thy brother, suffer it now, brother, that I may pull out the splinter out of thine eye, and, behold, a beam is in thine own eye? Thou hypocrite, first pull out the beam from thine own eye, and then shalt thou be able to see clearly to pull out the splinter out of thy brother's eye. Therefore whatsoever ye would that men should do to you, do ye even so to them: for this is the Law and the Prophets.

Be warned of false prophets, which come to you in sheep's clothing, but beneath their clothing they are as full of deceit as ravening wolves. But by their fruits ye shall recognise them. Are grape clusters gathered from thorns, or figs from thistles? Even so every good tree yieldeth good fruits, but every bad tree yieldeth bad fruits. A good tree cannot yield bad fruits, neither can a bad tree yield good fruits. But indeed every tree that yieldeth not good fruit is hewn down, and cast into the fire. And ye, by their fruits ye shall know them. Not every one that saith unto me, Lord, Lord, shall enter into the kingdom of Heaven; but him that doeth the will of my Father which is in heaven, the same shall enter with me into the kingdom of Heaven.

Whosoever heareth these my words, and doeth them, is likened unto a wise man, which built his house upon the rock; and the rain descended and the floods came and the winds blew, and beat upon that house: it fell not, for it was founded upon the rock. And whosoever heareth these my words, and doeth them not, is likened unto a foolish man, which built his house upon the sand; and the rain descended and the floods came and the winds blew upon it, and beat upon that house: it fell, and great was the fall of it.

CHAPTER IV

OPENING REMARKS: BLESSINGS AND WOES
(Matt. v. 3-12; Luke vi. 20-26)

The Lukan Version of the opening of the Speech is to be preferred to that in Matthew. It is direct. It is free from theological modifications of the unequivocal terms that Jesus used—the poor (in spirit), the hungry (for righteousness).

The purpose of the blessings and woes has already been indicated; it was to attract and attach the interest of the audience, the poor, the hungry, the mourning, and the despised. Jesus called them 'blissful.' Blissful, not in their present wretched state, but because their's is the Kingdom of God. A period is to be put to their unhappiness. The promised redemption is at hand. "God shall wipe away all tears from their eyes; and there shall be no more death, neither sorrow, nor crying, neither shall there be any more pain: for the former things are passed away" (Rev. xxi. 4). "Glad tidings to the poor and brokenhearted, beauty for ashes, the oil of joy for mourning, the garment of praise for the spirit of heaviness" (Isaiah lxi. 3).

How the pulse of the crowd must have quickened at the gracious words! How the people must have pressed closer, spellbound, to hear what would follow this propitious beginning! This much they would gather, that the Messiah was at hand to lift the iron heel of Rome from off their necks, and to punish the sinners in high places. They would also understand that for the Messiah's sake there would be persecution before the ultimate triumph: the tale of bricks would be more difficult to deliver before the second Moses could save his people.

Can it be doubted that the opening sentences of the Speech are Messianic? They reflect the comfortable visions of the ancient prophets and their successors the apocalyptists. Each sentence is a drop of balm on the wounded soul of Israel. Jesus echoes the author of *The Testaments of the Twelve Patriarchs*, who visions a time when:

> "They who have died in grief shall arise in joy,
> And they who were poor for the Lord's sake shall be made rich,
> And they who have been in want shall be filled,
> And they who have been weak shall be strong,
> And they who are put to death for the Lord's sake shall awake to life (*Test. of Judah* xxv. 4).

In the woes, the rich and well fed are to be understood as representing the Herodian princes and their set, the Sadducean priestly aristocracy and the wealthy landowners. "As in most countries of some degree of culture where many of the inhabitants have attained to means and even to wealth, so also in Palestine there were the superior 'breakers of the yoke,' scoffers and doubters, seeking only after pleasure and dissipation. Of such a type especially were the great landed proprietors, the rich men and merchants, certain members of the high priestly families, and most of the royal families who were in contact with the Greeks and Romans" (Klausner, *Jesus of Nazareth*, p. 196). Upon such the wrath of God would be poured out at the inauguration of the Messianic kingdom.

The closing chapters of the *Book of Enoch* are full of similar fulminations against the wealthy transgressors:

"Woe to you ye rich! for ye have trusted in your riches and from your riches ye shall depart, because ye have not remembered the Most High in the days of your riches. Ye have committed blasphemy and unrighteousness and have become ready for the day of slaughter and the day of darkness and the day of judgement.

"Woe to you sinners! for ye persecute the righteous; for ye will be delivered up and persecuted, ye people of injustice, and heavy will their yoke be upon you.

"Woe to you! who devour the finest of the wheat and drink the power of the source of the fountain, and tread under foot the lowly with your might" (ch. xciv.).

In voicing these sentiments Jesus was crying from the house-tops what the people had been accustomed to whisper in private; for Herod had initiated the system of "setting spies everywhere, both in the city and in the roads, who watched those who met together... and so find out what opinion they had of his government" (Antiq. XV. x. 4).

He spoke with authority, scorning the pseudonymity of the reformers among the Scribes and Pharisees. Matthew vii. 29 is usually explained as a reference to the rabbinic practice of giving weight to an opinion by quoting an earlier authority to the same effect; but this practice belongs to a later period. The meaning is, more probably, that Jesus did not, like the Pharisee writers of apocalypse, use the name of Israel's ancient worthies with which to cloak his revolutionary views. Here was a man who came out into the open, who smote the earth with the rod of his mouth and slew the wicked with the breath of his lips.

CHAPTER V

THE PERMANENCE OF THE LAW
(Matt. v. 17-20)

In the arrangement of the Speech here adopted, Jesus' statement about the permanence of the Law, and the necessity for keeping it in detail, follows immediately after the blessings and woes. The substance of the four verses omitted is found in other and more appropriate contexts (Mark ix. 50, xiv. 21; Luke viii. 16, xiv. 34).

The blessings and woes had been introductory to the Speech proper, which now begins. The Messiah's declaration is in the nature of the oath taken by the sovereign at his coronation that he will uphold the laws of the realm. At this very time in the popular expositions of the prophetic writings—Isaiah ix. 6-7 had been applied messianically, and the phrase "the government shall be upon his shoulder" had been rendered "he has taken the Law upon himself to keep it" (*Targum of Jonathan*).

In Order to understand why such a statement about the Law was necessary on the part of Jesus—why he had to put it in the very forefront of his address—it must again be emphasised that he was speaking to the commons of the nation. Since the heroic days of the Maccabees the Law had become the people's possession. They had died for it. They had realised in opposing the forces of Syro-Hellenism how vital it was to their national existence. The Law was no longer solely in the hands of the Scribes and pious priests; Seleucid tyranny and the multiplication of synagogues throughout the land had put an end to that. The peasantry were with the Pharisees 'separate' from the ungodliness of the ruling classes. The Law to them was the light "yoke of God's sovereignty." They had faith in the Mosaic ideal of "a kingdom of priests and a holy nation" which should be realised in the Messianic Age. They were ready at all times to risk their lives that the national life might be kept pure, and God's commandments carried out. They would pull down a golden eagle from the portals of the Temple, refuse to have an irreligious king such as Archelaus, join with a Judas of Galilee to resist a foreign census, or cast themselves by thousands on the ground and ask for death rather than that an Emperor's image should be set up in God's House (Antiq. XVII. vi. 2, xi. 1-2; XVIII. i. 1, viii. 1-6). For a Jewish leader of those days to have the support of the people, loyalty to the Law was the first essential.

There was some talk about a possible modification of the Law in the Messianic Age; but Jesus does not allow such an idea to be made a loophole for the lax-minded.

In asserting the permanence and binding quality of the Law, Jesus showed that he belonged to the People's party —the nationalists. Both for himself and for the populace the Law was a living creation composed like Paul's 'body of Christ' the Church, of many members—in this case precepts—more or less honourable, dependent on one another, and each necessary to the well-being of the whole.

THE PERMANENCE OF THE LAW

Popular parlance, which Jesus echoes, would have it that the smallest letter of the Hebrew alphabet and the little hooks which distinguished certain others would not pass away until the Law was kept by all. Then, of course, there would be no further need of the written code. By removing the hook of a letter of Scripture the sense could be changed from good to bad. For example the omission of a hook in the text of Leviticus xxii. 32 "Ye shall not profane my holy name" would change the sense to "Ye shall not praise my holy name" (Tanchuma, la). Hence the zealous Jewish guardianship of the sacred text. Weighty and light precepts were alike of God's giving. The penalty for breaking one of the least commandments was to be a low place in the Kingdom of God. Jesus would have subscribed heartily to the dictum of a famous second-century rabbi: "Be heedful of a light precept as of a weighty one, for thou knowest not the grant of reward for each precept" (Aboth ii.).

But Jesus rebuked certain of the Pharisees for their zeal for the least commandments and others of their own making while neglecting the weightier matters of the Law. There was the very real danger of losing the spirit in cleaving to the letter, of adding to the Law as well as taking away from it. Inward observance must accompany outward observance. For this was the day spoken of by Jeremiah the prophet (xxxi. 33), when God would make a new covenant with His people by writing His Law on their hearts. In this connection, in the Messianic discussions of the period, Psalm xcv. was frequently quoted:

"To-day if ye will hear his voice,
Harden not your heart
As in the provocation,
As the day of temptation in the wilderness:
When your fathers tempted me,
Proved me
And saw my work...
Unto whom I sware in my wrath,
Shall they enter into my rest.

"To-day if ye will hear my voice." The redemption could come immediately if Israel was obedient. "If all Israel would repent one day the Messianic Age would dawn," said the rabbis (Pal. Taanith, 42a). While the writer of the *Epistle to the Hebrews* (iii. 7-iv. 3) urges Christians to "Take heed lest there be in any of you an evil heart of unbelief in departing from the living God. But exhort one another daily, while it is called To-day; lest any of you be hardened through the deceitfulness of sin... Let us therefore fear, lest, a promise being left us of entering into his rest, any of you should seem to come short of it."

Jesus was striking a responsive chord in the hearts of his hearers in appealing for a more spiritual, single-minded devotion to the Law, without which entrance into the Kingdom of God was impossible. This was a fundamental requisite for the hastening of the promised Deliverance.

CHAPTER VI

CONCERNING MURDER
(Matt. v. 21-24)

This section of the Speech and the two that follow explain the statement about the Law which Jesus had just made. He now proceeds to illustrate his principles from the three commandments which the Jewish religious leaders in the stress of the times had lain down as fundamental. Again and again these three, concerning Murder, Adultery and Oaths, are grouped together, although Oaths is broadened to Idolatry. Thus: "Any sin denounced by the Law may be committed by a man if his life is threatened, except the sins of idolatry, adultery and murder" (Sanhed., fol. 64a); "Captivity comes upon the world on account of idolatry, adultery and murder" (Aboth v.); "Whoso slandereth his neighbour committeth sins as great as idolatry, adultery and murder" (Erech, fol. 15b). The Apostolic view was the same (Acts xv. 29) where the Gentile Christians are commanded to keep "these essential things; that ye abstain from things sacrificed to idols, and from blood, and from fornication" (Western Text).

We are now concerned with the Messiah's comment on the commandment "Thou shalt not murder." This crime was very prevalent in Palestine at this period. Josephus writes, "And now Judea was full of bands of robbers, and as the several companies of the seditious lit upon any one to head them, he was created a king immediately, in order to do mischief to the community. They did some small harm to a few of the Romans, but their murders of their own people lasted the longest" (Antiq. XVII. x. 8). Josephus was not in sympathy with the nationalists, and deliberately identifies them, as in this place, with the *banditti* who took ad-vantage of the disturbed state of the country to indulge in orgies of robbery with violence. It was the same anti-nationalist attitude which prompted the execution of Jesus, the patriot leader, between two such brigands.

It is noteworthy that about this time the Sanhedrin (composed very largely of friends of Rome) easily submitted, if it did not actually Petition, to be deprived of its power to judge in capital cases. The council of the Priests was glad enough to be freed from the responsibility of putting Jewish murderers to death, as among them would be many whose actions sprang from purely patriotic motives such as Judas of Galilee and his followers. Security with loss of dignity was preferable to the risk of popular vengeance. Inconvenient fire-brands might still be secretly apprehended and tried, but Rome would bear the blame for their execution. Thus reasoned the crafty leaders of the high-priestly party. The Sanhedrin of two generations earlier had been more courageous: they had been quite ready to condemn to death no less a dignitary than Herod himself, before he became king, for the massacre of the nationalist leader Hezekiah and his band, in spite of the fact that he presented himself before the judges attended by an armed bodyguard (Antiq. XIV. ix. 3-5).

"Forty years before the Temple was destroyed," says the Talmud, "judgement in capital cases was taken away from Israel" (Sanhed., fol. 24b). And again, "Forty years before the Temple was destroyed, the council removed (from the Hall of Hewn Stones in the Temple area) and sat in the Bazaars (just outside the hallowed precincts)" (Aboda Zara, fol. 8b). In Jewish tradition this removal of the council from its habitual place of session and the cessation of its power to judge capital cases are linked together. "They saw murderers so much increase," suggests R. Nachman bar Isaac, "that they were unable to condemn them. They said, therefore, 'It is fit that we should remove from place to place, that so we may avoid the guilt' (Ibid.). Elsewhere the Talmud tells us that owing to the enormous increase in the number of murderers, atonement for uncertain murders had ceased" (Soteh, fol. 47a).

At the time when Jesus was speaking life was held very cheaply, human relationships were strained to the breaking point—the natural consequence of overstrained nerves due to the unsettled and distressful state of affairs. The utterance of an angry or slanderous word was often followed by terrible consequences. The betrayal of a murderous spirit was tantamount to the actual commission of the capital crime. It was more than ever important, if redemption was to come, that the people should "preserve the unity of the spirit in the bond of peace." They must not profane God's House by going there to offer their gifts while harbouring thoughts of evil against their brethren.

It was sane advice that Jesus was giving; in fact it was an earnest plea for sanity under conditions which might well drive the meekest and mildest to extremes. Others besides Jesus had seen the danger and lifted up a warning voice:

"Unless ye keep yourselves from the spirit of lying and of anger, and love truth and long-suffering, ye shall perish. For anger is blindness, and does not suffer one to see the face of any man with truth" (Test, of Dan ii. 1-2).

"For the spirit of hatred worketh together with Satan, through hastiness of spirit, in all things unto men's death; but the spirit of love worketh together with the Law of God in long-suffering unto the salvation of men" (Test, of Gad iv. 7).

The rabbinical teaching is to the same effect. "Be as eager to secure thy fellow's honour as thine own; and yield not easily to anger" (Aboth v.).

"He that hath cause to be angry with his fellow, and is silent, shall be avenged by Him, who inhabiteth eternity" (Guittin, fol. 7a).

It can be seen how emphatic the teaching of Jesus was on this point, when in the early Hebrew Gospel Jerome records that it was placed among the greatest sins "if a man have grieved the spirit of his brother." And in *The Teaching of the Twelve Apostles* it is written: "Be not prone to anger, for anger leadeth to murder; nor given to party spirit, nor contentious, nor quick-tempered; for from all these things murders are generated" (iii. 2).

CHAPTER VII

CONCERNING ADULTERY
(Matt. v. 27-28)

The next commandment which Jesus brings forward in illustration of his principles of righteousness through which the goal of freedom is to be obtained is that concerning adultery. It is probable that in the original Speech his statement on this question was confined to one brief and emphatic sentence. The additional verses appear to have been spoken on other occasions.

The plague of vice temporally checked by the Maccabean reformation had broken out afresh in the Land of Israel. Territorial barriers could not stem the rising tide of corruption which was already engulfing the heathen world. It was indeed "a wicked and adulterous generation" to which Jesus was delivering his message. The lewd speech and practices of the citizens of Jerusalem had become proverbial (Shabbath, 62b). Morals were so lax that R. Jochanan ben Zaccai, soon after the time of which we are writing, ordered the cessation of the ordeal by bitter waters (Numbers v. 11-31), basing his action on Hosea iv. 14: "I will not punish your daughters when they commit whoredom, nor your spouses when they commit adultery" (Soteh, fol. 47a).

Contemporary writers spare neither priests nor people in their outspoken denunciations of national depravity. That generation was like the generation of the flood and like the inhabitants of Sodom and Gomorrah. A righteous God would mete out a similar judgement. The chief priests are depicted as "joining themselves with harlots and adulteresses, puffed up because of their priesthood, lifting themselves up against the commandments of God and men, contemning the holy things with jests and laughter" (Test, of Levi xiv. 5-6). High priests like Ishmael ben Phabi who went to offer sacrifice in a robe of such fine linen that it scarce concealed his nakedness. The monied classes are described as "committing adultery with their neighbours' wives, treading God's Sanctuary in all their pollutions, leaving no sin which they did not commit, even worse than the Gentiles" (Psalms of Solomon viii. 8-14).

The apostle Paul certainly had the mind of his Master and of every moral Jew when he wrote "that no whoremonger, nor unclean person... hath any inheritance in the kingdom of the Messiah and of God" (Eph. v. 5). Personal holiness is demanded of all who would have a part in the Redemption. "He that hath a pure mind in love, looketh not after a woman with a view to fornication; for he hath no defilement in his heart, because the Spirit of God resteth upon him" (Test, of Ben. viii. 2). These very words of a writer who lived a few years earlier than Jesus may have been in his mind when he spoke. Another Jewish teacher, a little later than he, could say: "He that committeth adultery with his eyes is also to be called an adulterer" (Lev. Rabba xxiii.).

The moral situation as Jesus found it was heart-breaking, but had not God promised to wash away the foulness from the daughters of Zion, to sprinkle clean water upon the people, that they might be unto Him a kingdom of priests and a holy nation. By the grace of God that nation would be born—born in a day—as the prophets had foretold.

CHAPTER VIII

CONCERNING OATHS
(Matt. v. 33-37)

The Messiah's application of the last of the triad of fundamental commandments is at first sight the most difficult to understand. So much so, that those who have ignored the topical character of the Speech have persistently misinterpreted his meaning. We have already noted that where Jesus alludes to swearing the religious leaders of his day speak of idolatry. It is not difficult to show that the same idea was in the mind of both.

With heathendom at the very gates it had become increasingly necessary to preserve the Name of God from profanation. The people constantly hearing their neighbours swear by Zeus, by the Capitoline Jove, and their other divinities, might easily be led to use the Name of the God of Israel as lightly. Pronunciation of the Tetragrammaton was therefore restricted to the Temple, where the priests, and at length only the high priest, might make mention of the Name with becoming reverence. In the provinces the priests and people were to substitute the title Adonai (the Lord), and then only when engaged in worship. The solemnity which attended the pronunciation of the Tetragrammaton appears in the impressive Jewish ritual for the Day of Atonement, from which the following extract may be quoted: "And when the priests and the people who stood in the court (of the Temple) heard the glorious, tremendous, and ineffable Name proceed from the mouth of the high priest with sanctity and purity, they kneeled and prostrated themselves, falling on their faces, and saying, 'Blessed be the Name of His glorious kingdom, for ever and ever.'" That the Name of God may be honoured amongst men was the prayer of every pious Jew, and this became almost a formula as may be seen from the opening sentences of the Aramaic *Kaddish* and the so-called Lord's prayer.

(1)

"Magnified and hallowed be His great Name in the world which He created according to His will. May He reveal His kingdom in your life time, etc."

(2)

"Our Father which art in heaven, hallowed be Thy Name. Thy kingdom come. Thy will be done in earth as it is in heaven."

For private intercourse even Adonai was forbidden, and what Dalman calls "evasive or precautionary modes of referring to God" such as 'Heaven,' 'the Name,' 'the Place,' 'Power,' must be used. This practice is found in the Gospels in such expressions as 'the kingdom of Heaven,' 'the right hand of Power.' If, however, any metonym for the Godhead was employed as an oath, the vow was binding, and its breach constituted a profanation of God's Name. This applied equally when a man vowed by anything dedicated to God such as the sacrifices on the altar, or the gold in the Temple. The religious leaders of the time discouraged swearing, but in deference to popular weakness they allowed oaths to which no guilt of profanation attached. Among these they mention 'By Jerusalem!', 'By the Temple!', 'By the life of my head!'. The Talmud in one place even says, "If any adjure another by heaven or earth, he is not guilty" (Sheb. iv.).

Jesus, and many with him, felt that this was mere subterfuge. "Whether is greater," he asks, "the gold, or the Temple that sanctifieth the gold?... Whether is greater, the offering, or the altar that sanctifieth the offering?" (Matt, xxiii. 16-22). "Swear not at all"; Jesus says in the Speech, "neither by heaven; for it is God's throne: nor by the earth; for it is His footstool: neither by Jerusalem; for it is the city of the great king." If Jews swore by these things, the heathen, who were prone to worship and serve the created thing rather than the Creator (Rom. i. 25), might suppose that they too were polytheists, and so even by what seemed harmless oaths God's Name would be profaned. The writer of 2 *Enoch* forbids swearing "by heaven or earth or any other created thing" (xlix. 1-2), and this was the general attitude towards oaths of the more spiritually minded. Josephus says of the Essenes that "Whatever they say also is firmer than an oath; but swearing is avoided by them, and they esteem it worse than perjury; for they say that what cannot be believed without swearing by God, is already condemned" (Wars II. vii. 6). To the same effect is Jesus the son of Sirach:

"Accustom not thy mouth to an oath;
And be not accustomed to the naming of the Holy One.
For as a servant that is continually scourged shall not lack a bruise,

So he also that sweareth and nameth God continually
shall not be cleansed from sin.":..
There is a manner of speech that is clothed about with
death;
Let it not be found in the heritage of Jacob"
(Ecclus xxiii. 9-12).

For all right-thinking men and women, simple asservations such as 'yes' and 'no' have the force of an oath, and no confirming word was required (Sheb., fol. 36a).

It may be understood that some Jews were very lax in the matter of swearing from the fact that it was found necessary to forbid partnership with a heathen "lest at any time he imposes an oath upon him (the Jew), and he is obliged to swear by his idol; and the Law says (Exod. xxiii. 13), 'Make no mention of the name of other gods, neither let it be heard out of thy mouth'" (Sanhed., fol. 63b).

We must therefore understand Jesus' condemnation of swearing not only on the ground of its impropriety, but because it was indirectly countenancing idolatry and consequently incompatible with a living faith in the sovereignty of God.

There is another aspect of the subject which cannot have been absent from the mind of Jesus. The taking of oaths had a political bearing. "Among the Romans," writes Edward Holton James, "oaths were considered of great importance and sanctity. The Roman policy was to make the subject peoples bind themselves to support the imperial government as securely as oaths could bind them... It was the custom of the subject peoples, in taking these oaths, to swear by those objects or places which they held in greatest veneration" (*Trial before Pilate*, pp. 45-46). To a loyal Jew, the taking of an oath of allegiance to Caesar meant a denial of the sole sovereignty of God; it would be serving two masters, worse, it would be serving other gods, for: "At the time that Jesus lived, the Roman emperor was everywhere adored as a divinity by those peoples who had accepted with docility the imperial regime. The cult of the emperor was in essence the adoration of the principle of imperial authority... A document discovered in Ethiopia, bearing the date March 26, 7 B.C., begins in these words, 'To Caesar who reigns over the seas and continents, Jupiter who holds from Jupiter his father the title of liberator, master of Europe and Asia, star of all Greece, who lifts himself up with the glory of great Jupiter, saviour'" (James, *loc. cit.*, pp. 43-44). Such an oath was therefore out of the question. Jesus, on a critical occasion, had been pressed to recognise Caesar's authority by paying tribute, and made the famous two-edged reply "Render unto Caesar the things that are Caesar's, and to God the things that are God's." Theologians have usually interpreted this answer to mean that Jesus accepted Caesar's sovereignty. How far from the truth this is. The second clause nullifies the first: God's claim to sole sovereignty left no room for Caesar's. While appearing unexceptionable to his tempter Jesus' action was as contemptuous as it well could be. Here was a denarius; it bore Caesar's portrait TIBERIUS CAESAR DIVI, divine Caesar, give it back to him. Jesus was virtually flinging Caesar's money and his theistic claims in his face.

Josephus tells us that when Herod demanded an oath of allegiance to Rome and himself the faithful Pharisees flatly refused. "And when all the rest of the Jewish people gave assurance by oath of their goodwill to the emperor and to the king's government, these very men would not swear, who were upwards of six thousand" (Antiq. XVII. ii. 4). If Caesar had made no claims to divinity it would have been another matter, but the honour of God was concerned, and neither Jesus nor the sincere Pharisees would countenance the profanation of God's Name by swearing by a false god.

CHAPTER IX

RETALIATION
(Matt. v. 38-48; Luke vi. 27-36)

In Matthew this section of the Speech is divided into two parts, while in Luke there is no break. Matthew probably gives the correct sequence, although Luke often preserves the original sense.

With the sentiments here expressed the climax of the Messianic application of the Law is reached. Jesus has been enunciating the principles of righteousness which must govern the people if they are to be found worthy to be redeemed from their enemies. Now he seeks to dissuade them from attempting to forestall that redemption by any ill-advised act of retaliation. "The vision is yet for an appointed time," he would say, "but at the end it shall speak, and not lie; though it tarry, wait for it; because it will surely come" (Habak. ii. 3). Or, to use his own words: "Of that day and hour knoweth no man, no, not the angels of heaven, but my Father only... Watch therefore" (Matt. xxiv. 36-44). Meanwhile "the just shall live by his faithfulness" (Habak. ii. 4). This, indeed, has been the doctrine of pious Jews through all the weary centuries of exile.

It is necessary to deal with this section of the Speech at greater length than with others, not only because here Jesus reaches the peak of his peroration, but because his meaning has been the subject of the keenest controversy.

Was he advocating passive resistance to any kind of ill-usage? Did he favour neutrality in the presence of brutality? A common interpretation of his statements would make Christianity synonymous with cowardice.

Once again it is essential to emphasise that Jesus had in view a particular set of conditions which affected the bulk of his immediate audience. It cannot be observed too strongly that when he spoke of enemies he meant national enemies—those who were neither relatives, friends, nor fellow Jews. There might be some doubt as to who was intended if the term had been 'neighbour'; but 'enemy' unquestionably stood for Rome and her Syro-Greek allies. Caesarea, the Roman Procurator's headquarters, was opposed to Jerusalem, the city of the great king. "If any one should tell thee that both cities are destroyed, believe him not; if he say both are peopled, again believe him not. If he say, Caesarea is destroyed and Jerusalem is peopled, or Jerusalem is destroyed and Caesarea is peopled, then believe him." So ran the Jewish proverb (Meg. 6a). When the political conditions in Palestine are given their due weight in the interpretation of the Messiah's teaching, much that is to-day obscure becomes pregnant with meaning.

As a guide to the situation with which Jesus is now dealing, we may quote from an excellent description by Dr. Klausner.

"There were aroused among the people of this time strong messianic longings which found expression in many *Apocryphal Books* filled with messianic fantasies and apocalyptic visions. The Sadducees, like the wealthy and aristocratic of all ages and nations, were thorough realists and saw that there was no hope of freeing themselves from Roman rule, and that their own position was not so bad as to be unendurable; and even the Pharisees were wise enough to recognise that 'vain is the help of man' and that all that they could look forward to was the mercy of heaven when in its good time it should see fit to send the righteous redeemer to Israel.

"But very different were the younger people, the hot-blooded and enthusiastic, who collected together in parties of 'zealots' whose object was to hasten the redemption and 'bring near the end.' From one end to the other Palestine was filled with malcontents and the rebellious-minded, and especially was this the case in Galilee, the cradle of 'Zealotism.' This is a fact which should not go unobserved in the history of Jesus. Also in Judaea and Jerusalem the great majority were weary of the heavy burden of the 'kingdom of Edom'—in both of its meanings. And once a people is 'weary of enduring' we can expect considerable political changes, for in those conditions the restless multitudes seize the first suitable moment for uprooting the existing order.

"Scarcely, indeed, had Herod closed his eyes than there immediately broke out such tumults and riots as the Jews had never before witnessed. ...All Judaea was, indeed, out of control. There was no ruler whose position was confirmed and who was accepted by the people; the smouldering hatred against the Edomite-Roman rule burst out like a volcano, and from one end of the country to the other were riots and disorders, tumult and confusion" (*Jesus of Nazareth*, pp. 158-155).

Jesus was opposed to the extreme zealots who would take the kingdom of Heaven by violence. He realised that all attempts to hasten the redemption must inevitably fail. He believed that God would directly intervene when the time was ripe. His policy of non-violence is governed by and has special relation to this idea. It was his own class, the peasantry, who suffered most, and who consequently were most disposed to retaliate. Many of them had already taken to the mountains and were waging a guerilla warfare on their enemies. They had lost everything and were utterly reckless and desperate.

Under the circumstances it was a difficult policy to advocate, this policy of No Reprisals. The people were at the mercy of the legionaries, many of them mercenaries —Syro-Greeks—whose hatred of the Jews was traditional, and who subjected the peasantry to every petty annoyance which they could devise. "What shall we do?" say the sarcastic soldiers to John the Baptist. "And he said unto them, Terrorise no man, neither bring false accusations; and be satisfied with your wages" (Luke iii. 14).

Jesus specifically mentions several of these acts of terrorism, and when his allusions are understood, it will be realised that it would indeed be 'perfection' in any people to remain quiescent under such provocation.

Imagine the sufferings of the poor Jewish peasant as Jesus describes them! At any moment rude legionaries may burst into his hovel to plunder his few possessions, brutally striking him if he resist (Matt. v. 39). If he has nothing else worth taking they will even strip him of his one coat (*chaloq*), leaving him only his outer robe (*talith*) to cover his nakedness (Matt. v. 40). There is no mention in Luke's Version of any legal proceedings in this connection (vi. 29). As he passes along the road with his donkey he may meet a company of Roman soldiers, and be compelled to carry their baggage for miles in the opposite direction to which he is going (Matt. v. 41). The very word for this forced service was Hebraised from the Greek, so that the *angaria* 'impressment' was spoken of with sullen hatred. Requests for money, and borrowing with no intention to repay was another of the afflictions the poor peasant had to endure (Matt. v. 42; Luke vi. 30): his little savings must all go to satisfy the rapacity of the avaricious mercenaries. That no question of charity was involved is made clear by the quotation in the *Teaching of the Twelve Apostles* (i. 4), which completes the sentence as it no doubt stood in the original: "If any one take from thee what is thine, ask it not back, for neither canst thou."

It is noteworthy that Jewish tradition attributes the destruction of Jerusalem to just such acts of retaliation as he would fain prevent. Several instances are quoted of which the following are typical. The people of a certain place had a custom to carry a cock and a hen before a bridal procession as symbols of procreation and fecundity. One day some Roman soldiers took away the cock and the hen, and being assaulted by the outraged members of the party, accused the Jews of rebellion against Caesar, with the result that troops were sent to quell the supposed rising. Again, there was a custom in another place to plant a cedar tree at the birth of a boy, and a pine tree at the birth of a girl. When a marriage took place the memorial trees of the bride and bridegroom were felled, and the wood used to construct their wedding canopy. One day the daughter of a Roman official (the text says the emperor) was travelling that way when the axle-tree of her carriage broke. Her attendants went and cut down what unfortunately happened to be one of these memorial trees in order to repair the damage. The Jews attacked them, and on this account were accused of rebellion and summarily dealt with (Gitt., fol. 57a).

The counsel which Jesus gave arose from his deep concern for his peoples' welfare. He could see that reprisals would only aggravate their unhappy condition. Let them instead endeavour to remove all rancour from their hearts, and even attain to the godlikeness of loving their enemies, that so their more speedy deliverance might be assured. At a later time, when Israel's sufferings were still acute, their spiritual heads endeavoured to inculcate the same lesson: "Be rather the object of curses than curse thyself" (Shabb., fol. 55a): "A man should always be among the persecuted rather than among the persecutors; for of birds, none are so persecuted as turtledoves and pigeons, and yet Scripture has designated them as an offering on the altar" (Aboda Zara, fol. 93a): "They who being reviled revile not again, who take no heed of insults, and act out of love, rejoicing in affliction, of them Scripture says, 'Them that love him are as the sun when he goeth forth in his might'" (B. Kama, fol. 93a).

That 'excess' of love and well-wishing for which Jesus pleads would make his hearers children of God indeed, and mete for deliverance.

CHAPTER X

PUBLIC DEMONSTRATION OF PIETY
(Matt. vi. 1-8, 16-18)

The construction of this section of the Speech again reveals the Hebraic mould of the Messiah's mind. Just as in an earlier passage of his dis course he had grouped his remarks concerning the Law around the fundamental commandments of his day—idolatry, adultery and murder—so now he speaks of piety under the three forms in which Judaism enjoined its practice—alms-giving, prayer and penitence (fasting). As Dr. Edersheim has rightly said, "Fasting and prayer, or else fasting and alms, or all the three, were always combined. Fasting represented the negative, prayer and alms the positive element, in the forgiveness of sins" (*Life and Times of Jesus*, vol. I., p. 662). The sentiment is found already in Tobit: "Good is prayer with fasting and alms and righteousness" (xii. 8). But we have the definite dictum of Judaism in the statement of R. Eliezer: "Three things cancel the harsh decree of Heaven, prayer, alms-giving and penitence" (Y. Taan., fol. 2a). The equation fasting-penitence is a very ancient one. Fasting was the outward expression of inward contrition. In Ecclesiasticus we have the phrase "fasting for sins" (xxxiv. 26), but it was always emphasised that fasting unaccompanied by change of heart was valueless.

This is well brought out in the description of the ceremony observed at the time of Jesus on public fast days. The ark containing the scrolls of the Law was brought out of the synagogue into the market-square of the town, and dust was sprinkled upon it, as also on the heads of the ruler of the synagogue and the president of the local Sanhedrin and of all the people. Then the eldest present spoke the following admonition to penitence, "My brethren, it is not said of the men of Nineveh, God saw their sackcloth and their fast, but 'God saw their works, that they turned from their evil way.' And in the Prophets, what saith it? 'Rend your hearts and not your garments, and turn to the Lord your God'" (Y. Taan., fol. 2a). At a later stage in his ministry, when a lack of response to his message was apparent, Jesus also exclaimed, "The men of Nineveh shall rise in the Judgement with this generation, and shall condemn it: because they repented at the preaching of Jonah; and, behold, a greater than Jonah is here" (Matt, xii. 41).

The connecting link with the previous section of the Speech is supplied by the thought of reward. Jesus had asked, What reward could faithful Jews expect if their conduct was no better than that of those who neither knew nor feared God? Now, lest his words be misunderstood, he hastens to explain that by 'doing more than others' he does not mean a public parade of piety: such behaviour would negative the heavenly reward. There were far too many of the type which "do all their works to be seen of men." They had their reward already in public adulation. An early Jewish tradition distinguishes seven kinds of Pharisee (Sota, fol. 22b), and of these, six come under condemnation. The second on the list, and perhaps also the fifth variety, was in the mind of Jesus when he issued his warning. These two are styled the 'book-keeping' Pharisee and the 'what-is-my-obligation-

and-I-will-do-it' Pharisee, the former presumably from the vainglorious habit of computing the amount of reward due for the performance of good deeds. The more self-sacrificing the deed the greater the reward. It was of this type that R. Judah the Prince said: "Be heedful of a light precept as of a grave one, for thou knowest not the grant of reward for each precept" (Aboth ii. 1). And there is the well-known rabbinical saying: "He who giveth alms in secret is greater than Moses our master" (B. Bathra, fol. 9b).

One can readily understand that at such a time of public calamity there were many devoted souls who gave themselves to prayer, fasting and alms-giving that God might look with favour on His people. These would have been ashamed to confess their vicarious atonement. One can as readily appreciate the temptation of less single-minded persons to let it be seen that they were interceding for the nation. The poor people in their desperate state would follow such with their blessings, assured that there must be a response from heaven to the pleas of these pietists.

A cento of quotations Biblical and non-Biblical could be given on the subject of reward which is the basis of the Messiah's statement, but suffice it to make clear what was in his mind. It had long been deduced from such passages as Isaiah xl. 10 and lxii. 11 that God's grant of reward to the righteous would be dispensed by the Messiah at his coming. R. Tarphon in the second century voices the popular belief: "The grant of reward unto the righteous will be in the Messianic age" (Aboth ii. 21). Jesus as Messiah would himself be the dispenser of the heavenly reward, as he says: "For the Son of Man shall come in the glory of his Father with his angels; and then shall he reward every man according to his works" (Matt. xvi. 27: cf. Rev. xxii. 12).

His audience stands before him as the people over whom he will one day rule, therefore there is the ring of authority in his voice as he issues his commands not to act hypocritically. Sitting on the mountain-side he sees himself in imagination seated on the Throne of Glory (Matt. xxv. 31): instead of the crowd standing below, all nations are gathered before him for judgement (Matt. xxv. 32): his twelve disciples at his feet are seated on lower thrones judging the twelve tribes of Israel (Matt. xix. 28). Of the nature of the reward Jesus does not speak; both for him and his contemporaries it was enough that "Eye hath not seen, nor ear heard, neither have entered into the heart of man, the things which God hath prepared for them that love him" (I Cor. ii. 9).

CHAPTER XI

FAULT FINDING
(Matt. vii. 1-5, 12; Luke vi. 37-38, 39-40)

The mind of the Messiah moves on from those who parade their piety to those who go about looking for small faults in others. Jesus warns his hearers against three types of persons, the ostentatious pietist, the fault finder and the false prophet. The essential point to remember is that behind each type is the insistent anxiety for deliverance. Those who "seemed to be somewhat" received the blessings of the people, sometimes unworthily, for hastening the Redemption by their holy lives, while others were praised for their seemingly pious reproofs of those whose conduct appeared to be retarding the Redemption. In the language of the day the transgressors were "causing the Shechinah (the Divine Presence) to depart from Israel."

Among no other nation can one find such continuous longing and anxiety for the consciousness of the presence of God as among the Jews. From the prayer of Moses, "If thy presence go not with us, take us not up hence" onwards, Jewish literature is full of such spiritual solicitude, and never more so than in the dark days which preceded and followed the destruction of the second Temple. Again and again there is mention of those whose pure lives made them worthy that the Divine Presence should rest upon them, and of those whose unworthy acts caused that Presence to depart in grief. Salvation itself depended on the measure in which God was with His people. He was their final refuge. All other help had failed. This is the real significance of the name Emmanuel (God-with-us) given to the Messiah: not God in the flesh of men, but the advent of the Messiah signified that God's presence was assured: "Blessed be the Lord God of Israel; for he hath visited and redeemed his people, and hath raised up an horn of salvation for us in the house of his servant David" (Luke i. 68-69).

Under these circumstances one can hardly wonder that brother should look on brother with a jaundiced eye, and that with some individuals the search for error in others amounted almost to a mania. The motive was well enough, but the state of mind was decidedly unhealthy. The Talmud aptly sums up the situation by saying that it was "a generation which judged its judges" (B. Bathra, fol. 15b), and quotes the same proverb as Jesus about the splinter and the beam.

What is especially noteworthy about this section of the Speech is Jesus' use of popular proverbs, and the compiler of Matthew having remarked this fact has thrown in a few more which Jesus had quoted at other times. It was the Messiah's common-sense way of dealing with the mental tension and nerviness. He deliberately lowers his tone to the colloquial, and eases the harshness of spirit by appealing to popular adages, the homely humour of the market-place. One must possess a very dry theology not to appreciate the fun of the splinter and the beam. Both this proverb and "With what measure a man metes, it shall be measured unto him again" (Sota, fol. 8b) were familiar to everyone.

Jesus deliberately draws the sting of the *unco' guid*, from whose activities he was to suffer continually. They dogged his footsteps, quibbling over his eating with publicans and sinners, over his disciples eating without the ritual hand-washing, over their plucking ears of corn on the Sabbath. Such men make mountains out of molehills, tremendous issues out of trivialities. They make for schisms and factions. They are liable to wreck any large movement.

The famous Rabbi Hillel, an elder contemporary of Jesus, had once been asked by a heathen would-be proselyte to Judaism to teach him the whole Law while he stood on one leg. Said the meek and patient Hillel, "What is hateful to thee, do not unto others. This is the Law, the rest is commentary."

"The rest is commentary," Jesus agrees, and turns the old rabbi's saying round to a positive commandment. If the people will spend them-selves in doing good to others, they will have no time to go fault finding and heresy hunting.

CHAPTER XII

FALSE PROPHETS
(Matt. vii. 15-21; Luke vi. 43-46)

From other places in the Gospels we know that the people presented the picture to Jesus of sheep without a shepherd. Apart from himself, there does not stand out in the history of the time the figure of any great popular leader, who could gather around him all the diverse elements, the perishing sheep of the house of Israel. There were groups and factions, petty chieftains who had their hour, religious enthusiasts who preached messages of hope but did little to realise the hopes they raised.

On the other hand there were the wolves in sheep's clothing, battening on the people's misery. Jesus has been speaking of the fault finders, one disruptive element which tended to promote divisions instead of unity. Now he warns against a definitely destructive element, those ghouls who, taking advantage of the distraught and helpless, promised to a longing and expectant nation, believers in the miraculous, signs and wonders which were to presage the Redemption.

Among the Samaritans "there was one who thought lying of little consequence, and who contrived everything to please the multitude. So he bade them assemble together upon Mount Gerizim, which is by them looked upon as the most holy of all mountains, and assured them, that when they came there, he would show them the sacred vessels that were buried there, because Moses had put them there" (Jos. Antiq. XVIII. iv. 1).

"When Fadus was procurator of Judaea, a certain imposter, whose name was Theudas, urged a great part of the people to take their effects with them, and follow him to the river Jordan; for he told them that he was a prophet, and that he would, by his own command, divide the river, and afford them an easy passage over it: and many were deluded by his words" (Antiq. XX. v. 1).

In Felix' time "there came out of Egypt to Jerusalem, one that said he was a prophet, and advised the multitude of the common people to go along with him to the Mount of Olives... for he said he wished to show them from thence, how, at his command, the walls of Jerusalem would fall down, through which he promised to procure them an entrance into the city" (Antiq. XX. vii. 6).

"A wicked and adulterous generation seeketh after a sign," Jesus sternly said, "and no sign shall be given unto it" (Matt. xvi. 4).

No miracle was too wonderful for the wretched and credulous multitudes to swallow, with the natural result that they became the prey of a host of charlatans. It is one of the great tragedies of history that the one who, above all, set his face steadfastly against any attempt to beguile the people by wonder-working, should have been condemned as a false prophet and misleader. "By their fruits ye shall know them," and that is his vindication. But no man saw more clearly the terrible danger, or did more to try and avert it. The Day of Deliverance rested with God alone; it was for those who wished to participate in it to prepare themselves by doing the will of God.

CHAPTER XIII

CONCLUSION: SIMILE OF THE BUILDERS
(Matt. vii. 24-27; Luke vi. 47-49)

The great Speech draws to its close. Into its brief compass Jesus has incorporated all that was of real import for the welfare of his people. No wonder that "the people were astonished at his teaching." Was not this the Messiah, upon whom the Spirit of God rested so completely?

He sums up in a parable with which in various forms his audience was familiar. "Elisha ben Abuyah saith: A man who has good works and has studied the Law greatly is like a man who buildeth stones below and bricks above, so that even though many waters may surge against the sides of the building, they cannot move it from its place. But a man who has no good works and has studied the Law is like a man who builds bricks first and stones upon them; even a little water upsets them at once" (Aboth d'R. Nathan xxiv.).

"R. Eleazar said in the name of R. Chanina, The disciples of the wise multiply peace in the world, as it is said, And all thy children shall be taught of the Lord; and great shall be the peace of thy children. Read not here *banayich*, thy children, but *bonayich*, thy builders" (Ber. concl.).

Jesus himself was the master-builder, and his teaching the rock upon which should be built the community of the Kingdom of God, and the very abyss of hell should not prevail against it. "Therefore thus saith the Lord God, Behold, I lay in Zion for a foundation, a stone, a tried stone, a precious corner stone, a sure foundation: he that believeth shall not be confounded" (Isaiah xxviii. 16).

Down the ages rings the message of the Speech on the Mount—the Speech that Moved the World —that will yet vitalise it into action that shall bring peace on earth and goodwill among men.

www.ingramcontent.com/pod-product-compliance
Lightning Source LLC
LaVergne TN
LVHW032013070526
838202LV00059B/6442